Chee
Me Boodies!

A Celebration of Devon Dialect

John Germon

with illustrations by Richard Scollins

COUNTRYSIDE BOOKS
NEWBURY BERKSHIRE

First published 2008

COUNTRYSIDE BOOKS
3 Catherine Road
Newbury, Berkshire

To view our complete range of books,
please visit us at
www.countrysidebooks.co.uk

ISBN 978 1 84674 120 3

Designed by Peter Davies, Nautilus Design
Produced through MRM Associates Ltd., Reading
Typeset by CJWT Solutions, St Helens
Printed by Cambridge University Press

*All material for the manufacture of this book
was sourced from sustainable forests*

CONTENTS

ACKNOWLEDGEMENTS

Both Publisher and Author acknowledge with gratitude the debt they owe to *Ey Up Mi Duck!* by Richard Scollins and John Titford, first published in 1976. That book was the inspiration for the series of regional dialect volumes, of which this is one.

* * * *

Personal thanks go to the Oracle at Exeter and to the Widecombe History Society. For more details on Widecombe, visit www.widecombe-in-the-moor.com

I would also like to acknowledge the enjoyable times spent with the members of the Ashburton Devon Dialect Club sharing and helping to preserve our Devon dialect over the past twenty odd years.

VOREWARD

'Hello my boodies, 'ow be knackin' vore?' (How are you getting on?)

You will find in Devon that there are many variations of dialect and words: north, south and east all have their variations. Equally, throughout Devon, Cornwall, Dorset and Somerset the borders are no barriers to dialect and that is why you will often hear familiar words in each county. Of course, as far as I am concerned, being prejudiced, Devon has the correct words and we have just lent them to other counties – although I expect they would disagree!

As well as the true Devon dialect words, we have to take into consideration local pronunciation and regional accents, and you will also get differences in grammatical construction.

I remember one particular word that I mentioned on BBC Radio Devon – GRUTUS, which is the name for the part of a plough that turns the furrow. I received a huge response, offering a lot of variations, along with the usual 'You gurt mump aid, you 'eve got 'n wrong, tid'n the word fer thikky part.' Some of the alternatives were GRIDUS, GRAWDIS and GROOTUS. Investigating further, it has been suggested that the original term was in fact GROOT REST, groot (untilled soil) being put to rest (turned), with the rest of the words being a corruption of this.

Another interesting illustration is the variety of names for a foxglove, used in different areas of Devon: FLOPPYDOCK, COWFLOP (these are the two most common) followed by PROUD LADIES, MOUNTAIN TULIPS, FAIRY THIMBLES and so on.

Then one has to be aware of differences in the pronunciation of letters. You will notice, for example, that *s* can become *z*; *f* is often *v*; *o* is sometimes changed for *a*; *oo* will often sound like *u*:

Sunday – Zunday or Zinday
Summer – Zummer
Sand – Zand
Fast – Vast
Farmer – Varmer
Fish – Veesh

Fool – Vool or Vule
Stop – Stap
Proper – Praper or Praaper

I am often asked how to write in Devon dialect. This does create problems because there have been deviations from the original dialect words, plus various areas of the county say the words differently so I can only suggest that they would have spelt them as they hear them. I suppose the answer to that question is: 'You write it as you yer it.'

I have no doubt that some people may disagree with certain words in this book, saying that is not how it is spelt or not as it is said – or indeed that it is not a true Devon word. I certainly do not claim to be an expert, only someone who has a fascination with the Devon dialect and the county generally, agreeing totally as I do with the assertion 'Deb'm be eb'm on earth'.

There are very many words to look at and I have only been able to include a fraction of them in this book. I hope, though, that my selection will help towards edifying you in th' Deb'm dialect. My thanks goes to 'The Oracle' of Exeter who has sent me many letters on the subject; I am unable to tell you who this is as the writer has never given me their name or address – but I am grateful to you, whoever you are.

I hope you enjoy the book and find it of some use, as well as a source of amusement. Do not be afraid to try some of the words or sayings – have a go at them as it will show people that you do know how to talk praaper like what uz do!

'Cheers me boodies 'n uz'l zee 'ee dreckly.'

John Germon

CHAPTER 1

A Deb'm Dictionary

ABROAD — Broken to pieces
'Look at th' ole cloam pot, 'ee've scat 'n abroad.'

ACE, ISS, AYS — Yes
'Oh ays, it do zute uz to zay uz be or else uz baint.'

AIMZES, AMEZES — Hames (part of a horse's collar)
'Zort out thikky aimzes will 'ee, they'm lookin' a bit raimid [stretched]*.'*

ANGLEDUG, ANGLETWITCH — Common earthworm

ANKERCHER — Handkerchief

ANSTEEVE — Handle of a flail
'This yer ansteeve be proper ramshackled [rickety]*.'*

APPLEDRANE — Wasp
'Will 'ee mop up thikky trade, else 'twill draw th' ole appledranes to 'ee.'

APSE — Hasp, fasten
'Why dawnt 'ee apse thikky door 'n a proper manner, yer gurt mump aid!'

ARRISH — Stubble – when a field has been cut you are left with the stubble

A-VEERED — Afraid
'Look at th' gurt gawk, 'ee be a-veered o' a little ole appledrane.'

AVORE — Before

AXWADDLER — Ash peddler – someone who collected wood or peat ash to be used in the manufacture of soap

BACK-ZE-VORE Back to front
'Yer gurt gawk, yer vest be back-ze-vore.'

BAINT *'Uz baint'* – We are not
'Baint right' – It is not right

BATCHELOR'S BUTTONS
Old name for the burdock plant

BELLERZIZ, BELLAZIZ
Bellows
'If you want a tune out o' thikky orgin maister, you 'ad better give thikky bellaziz a master pumpin', else uz'l end up with nort.'

BELVE Shout or sing loudly
'Listen t' thikky cheel belve.'

BILLERS Hollow stems of plants such as cow parsley

BIRD'S EYE Speedwell

BISHOP'S WEED Ground elder

BISSLY, BISSLE Beastly, dirty
'Get rid o' th' bissly ole thing will 'ee?'

BLACKAID Tadpole

BLACK ARMY Fleas

BLADDERS Blisters – Jan Stewer in one of his famous books wrote that he had *'bladders on both veet 'n was pummel vooted ver a vortnight.'*

BLESS VORE A 'charm' or spell usually used to cure disorders such as warts, ringworm, etc

BLIDDY WARRIORS
This is a very old Devon name for wallflowers – it is said that they are called this because they resemble lines of warriors in bright tunics!

BLOOTH, BLOATH Blossom, bloom
'Caw, kin 'ee zee th' blooth on th' ole tree.'

BRANDY BOTTLE Yellow waterlily

BREAD 'N CHEESE Hawthorn leaves and berries

BRIMMLES, BRIMBLES
Brambles
'You watch yer 'ands buye, they ole brimbles'l scratch 'ee t' bits.'

BROKEN MOUTHED
Without teeth
'This yer 'oss be master broken mouthed.'

CAUCHY, COOCHY Left handed
'Look at 'ee with thikky dart, 'ee be proper coochy handed.'

CHAWK, CHAUK Jackdaw

CHEAL, CHEEL This usually relates to girls (as buyes be buyes); a young cheel, or young maiden, who will grow up to be an 'ooman

CHILLERN Children
'Will 'ee look at they chillern, they be jumpin' up 'n down like a bag o' flays [fleas]*.'*

CHIKKY Cheeky
'Chikky varment – if you ask me 'ee needs a good thraipin.'

CHITTERLINS Pigs' intestines
Also used in connection with humans:
'Doctor me chitterlins be all back-ze-vore'

CHONCHABLES Icicles

CLAUVELL, CLAWVIL Beam of wood over the top of a fireplace

CLAW AMMER COAT Tail coat

CLEDGY, CLAGGY, CLADGY
Sticky, muddy, claylike
'Dawnt 'ee go vallin' een there buye, 'tiz master cledgy.'

CLOAM — Made of earthenware or clay, as in '*cloam omn*' [oven]'

COCKLEERT — Dawn
It has been suggested to me that this could be related to when the cock bird is alert (Pass!)

CONFUDDLED — Confused

COOSE — This is the iron tip on hobnail boots

COWFLOPS, FLOPPYDOCKS
Foxgloves

CRACKETY, CRACKY-WRAN, KRACKETTY
Wren
'Caw kin 'ee yer th' ole crackety, her be soundin' boodiful.'

CRADDED — Of acid disposition
'I tell 'ee, maister be proper cradded smornin'.'

CRILLY GREENS — Curly greens, curly kale

CRUMPIDDY — Uncomfortable, awkward
'O get away with 'ee, you be proper crumpiddy like.'

DAWBAKE — Person who is stupid
'Git out o' yer, yer gurt dawbake.'

DAYCHIN' — Thatching
'Jan was busy at 'ees work a daychin' 'n a ditchin'.'

DEESH WASHER — Wagtail

DEEVE — Deaf
''Tiz no good spaikin' t' 'ee. Ee's deeves a pawst.'

DEW SNAIL — A slug
'Jist git a scat o' rain 'n th' ole dew snails be all auver th' plaace.'

DIMPSY, DIMMETT
Twilight – just as the sun has faded and it is starting to get dark, *'tiz zaid t' be gettin' dimpsy.*

DIP CHICK — Moorhen

DOLLOP — Measure
'Git on me boody, trait yerzel 'n eve a gurt dollop o' craame.'

DONNIKIN — This was the name given to the earth privy that you would find at the bottom of the garden or across the yard. I remember being amazed at how small my Grandfather's

	newspapers used to be in the donnikin, and how strange it was storing them on a bit of string
DOWEL	The Devil
DRANGWAY	Narrow passageway, alley *''Ee jist rinned up thikky drangway.'*
DRECKLY, DREKLY	Later on Cornwall will always tell you that this word is Cornish. Devonians will always tell you that the word is Devonian!
DREXIL, DRECKSILL	Threshold, doorstep *'Eb'm got time t' stop 'n yap me boody, I got t' git out 'n scrub th' ole drexil.'*
DRUMBLE DRANE	Bumblebee *''Twaz ummin' jist like a drumble drane on a floppydock.'*
DUG	Dog (here in Ashburton the Red Lion Inn is always known as the 'Red Dug'!)

EDIFICATION	Education – the word is a mix between edify and education
EEN TU	Into *''Ee's a gurt mump aid, 'ee id'n gwain een tu 'n proper, praps 'tiz cuz 'ee id'n eezel.'*
'EE'S	He is, he's
EEZEL	Himself
ERBONS	Ribbons
EVIL	Fork
FANTY SHEENY	Absurdly fanciful *'They Zinday clothes 'er ad on was master fanty sheeny.'*
FERN TICKET	Permit Locally, we tell Grockles that if they are going onto the moors, especially courting, they will need a fern ticket as you aren't allowed behind bushes with a maid unless you have one!
FINNIKY	Fussy *'Zome maid oo dawnt like rompin' 'n th' hay.'* Uz eb'm had any such problems yer in Ashburton!

FITCH	Polecat, ferret (and sometimes used for a weasel)
FLIBBERTS, FLITTERINS	Small pieces; an expression that I also like is flibberty skriddicks – bits and pieces
FLITTERMOUSE	Bat *'What was that? Purt near scat me one on thikky aid.' 'Aw 'twas jist 'n ole flittermouse.'*
FLOPPYDOCK	Foxglove
FLUMMOXED	Puzzled (see also '**Mizmaize**')
FRAWZY	Celebration, treat; it used to be that people would have a *wazegooze 'n frawzy*, which was an outing, ending up with a treat, something like *tay 'n pasty*
FUZPIG	Hedgehog; also sometimes known as hedgy boar, or the 'f' could be swapped for a 'v', making *vuzpig* (see also **Hedgy Boar**)

FUZZCHAT	Stonechat
GLEANIES	Guinea fowl *'I zeed thikky gleanies o'er yonder hill avore noon.'*
GODS O' MIGHTY COW	Ladybird
GOLDEN GLADDY	The yellowhammer bird
GOO'COOS	Bluebells
GOOD FER NORT	Good for nothing *'That gurt guzzle guts be good fer nort, 'Ee's es much good es a dog with zide pockets.'*

GOOZE GOBS Gooseberries; also known as *gooze gogs*
'Do uz a faver maid will 'ee, go out 'n git uz zome gooze gobs.'

GRANFER GRIGG Woodlouse; also sometimes known as a ***zowpig*** or ***zowpeg***
Best place I have found for granfer griggs is in old moots. I have also been told that some people use this name for a long-legged water insect.

GRANNIE'S BONNET Columbine

GREY BIRD (bit like mezel!) Song thrush

GROCKLE Visitor
This is a fairly recent term, but has become very common, so I think that I have to include it. It has been suggested to me that there was once an entertainer called 'Grockle the Clown' who toured Devon and his face was made up with bright red makeup – this could be where the name comes from as tourists with their bright red sunburnt faces reminded local people of Grockle (I do not know if this is true but it is a nice story anyway). In Devon and Cornwall you will hear visitors also referred to as *emmets* – a much older word – which means 'ants', i.e. hundreds of them and they are all over the place!

GRUTUS The part of a plough that turns a furrow (see this book's **Voreward**)

GUZZLE GUTS Someone who drinks to extreme
'Yer, Maister, be nort but 'n ole guzzle guts.'

GWAIN Going
'Where be gwain me boody? If 'eed 'ev asked me I could o' told 'ee 'ee wuz lost!'

HANKERCHER Handkerchief (see also '**Ankercher**')

HARNZEE Heron

HAVAGE Ancestry

HEABLE Pitchfork
'Yer buye, take th' ole heable out 'n scat thikky straw about will 'ee.'

HECKAMAL, HAKAMAL, HECKYMAL
Tomtit

HEDGY BOAR Hedgehog (see also '**Fuzpig**')

HIKKETY A wooden latch on one side of a door

HOMESCREECH Mistlethrush
'A boodiful bird, bit like the Mother in law, dawnt 'ee knaw?'

HOOP Bullfinch

HORNYWINK Lapwing
'Dawn 'ee go shootin' 'ee buye, 'tiz only a hornywink.'

HUSSEY An implement for resting pans on in an open-hearth fire, usually attached to a crook.

ID'N 'EE Isn't he

INDERZIDE Underside

INJIN' Engine

INNERDS One's internal organs
''Ee's master fer takin' abroad th' innerds of th' ole injin', id'n 'ee? 'Ee loves gettin' all thikky bits out, specially inderzide, 'n if 'ee's lucky, they all go's back again purt viddy.'

JEWSIVE — Possibly a corruption of 'deuced' but present usage seems to be related to 'ever so large'
''Twas a jewsive pain, purt near knocked the brains out droo th' top o' me 'aid.'

JINGLE, JINGEL — A two-wheeled vehicle drawn by a pony or cob

JONNICK — Pleasant, agreeable, easy to get on with

KEE — Cow

KETCH VORE — Catch up with
'Uz ad better git a move on maid, if uz be gwain t' ketch vore.'

KICKSHAW — Amusement, entertainment, exhibition
'Caw, last yer's Carnival was a proper kickshaw.'

KIT — Buzzard

KITTY TOPE — Jenny wren

KURZMUS — Christmas

LEARY — Empty, unladen; sometimes also used for 'hungry'

LENT LILLIES, LENT ROSES — Wild daffodils; I have also heard them called *daffle down dillies*

LINNEY — Place where carts, wagons, tools, etc are kept; a favourite pastime was having to limewash the linney.

LONG DUG — Greyhound
'My gurd, ole Jan rinned up th' nap o' thikky hill like a long dug.'

LOUSTERIN', LOUSTER — Working hard/hard work
'Varmer would be out all day lousterin' a daychin' 'n a ditchin'.'

MAID, MAID'N — Teenage girl
A baby girl is known as a cheal; some people refer to baby boys or girls as 'cheal' – I have to say that I have always known a buye as a buye!

MAISTER — Mr

MAIZE, MAIZED — Daft, mad

MASTER — Used to describe something considered large
'Caw, they wuz a master crop o' teddies.'

MAUNDERIN' — Muttering, grumbling
'Th gurt vule, ee's always maunderin' to 'eez'el.'

MAY BLOOTH — Hawthorn

MAZZARDS, MAZZERDS — Damsons

MEZEL — Myself
'If you ask me, I kin tell 'ee I'd keep 'n to mezel.'

MIZMAIZE — Confused (see also **'Flummoxed'**)

MOMMET — Scarecrow
'Look at 'ee, 'ee looks a proper mommet.'

MOOT — Tree stump
'Take this yer vizgie 'n dig out thikky moot, will 'ee?'

MOOWAY, MOWHAY — Rickyard; stooks of corn would be stacked into ricks and stored in a mooway

MORT, MORT'L A lot, large
'Caw, 'twas a mort'l size I tell 'ee, me boody, I eb'm zin nort like it.'

MOUTH SPAICH Dialect, speech
'I tell 'ee buye, th' ole Deb'm dialect be th' only mouth spaich t' spaik.'

MUMCHANCE Mute, silent
There are certain times when I wish certain people was a bit mumchance!

MUMP AID, MUMP AIDED
Silly person/silly
You will also sometimes hear the expression *addle aided* – slow witted

MUTY ARTED Soft hearted, easily upset
''Er be jist muty arted, if truth wuz t' tell; 'er baint zo brave.'

MUZCRAWL, MUSCRAW, MASCALL Caterpillar

NACK/KNACK Knock
This word would be heard in the greeting *'Ow be nackin' vore?'* – How are you getting along, going forward?

NAMMET, NUMMET
According to 'The Oracle' in Exeter, this word is circa mid 1800s and relates to a mid morning snack – what us would term *lemzees*

NAP The top of, horizon
'Last time I zeed 'n 'ee wuz auver nap o' thikky hill.'

NATLINS Intestines
''Tiz no use drinkin' too much, cuz 'twill make yer natlins 'n yer kidleys all back-ze-vore.'

NIDDICK The nape (hollow) of the neck

NIMPINGANG A very old word for a whitlow

NISSLEDRAFT, NIZZLEDREDGE
The runt in a litter of pigs; and sometimes I have heard the letter 'm' used instead of 'n' – *missledraft*

NITTALS Hazel trees, bushes

NORNNY An old Devon word for Northenhay, Exeter

NORT, KNAW NORT
Nothing, know nothing
'Get out do, 'ee' s nort but 'n ole knaw nort.'

NUBBIES — Yeast buns flavoured with saffron

OOD — Wood
There's nort better than turning a nice bit o' 'ood on thikky lathe.

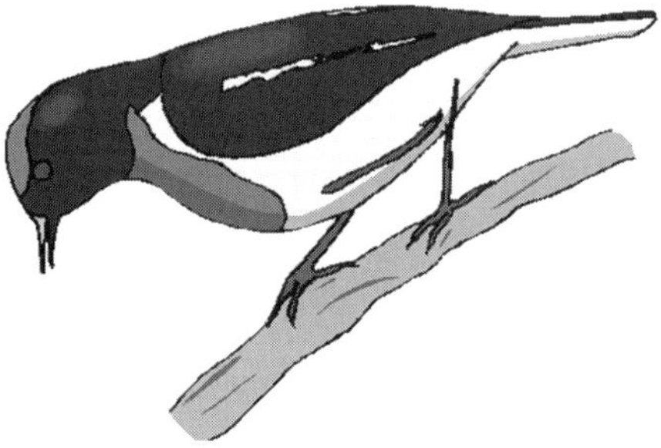

OOD-ALL, OODWALL
Woodpecker

OOZLE — Whistle, throat
'Come on me boody, 'tiz time t' nip down th' ole Red Dug [Red Lion] 'n wet yer oozle.'

ORNYWINK — Lapwing

ORT 'N NORT — Something and nothing
'Look at the size o' they teddies, 'tiz a bit o' ort 'n nort.'

ORTS — Odds, scraps
'Uz 'ed better give thikky orts t' th' ole dug.'

OSS — Horse

O'T — Of it
'I dawnt think nort o't [pronounced 'aw it'].'

PAIKE — Tardy person
Also I have heard it said that someone just poking about and not getting on with things is *'paiks'n 'bout doin' nort'.*

PAIKEN — To doodle

PAUCHED, PAUNCHED
Description of a field cut up by stock, making it boggy

PELLUM, PILLEM, PILLUM — Dust
'Dawnt 'ee go up thikky tallet, cuz you'll kick up th' pellum 'n 'twill make a master mess.'

PINSWELL — Small boil or abscess

PIXIE FLAX — Cotton grass

PIXIE LAID, PIXIE LAID'N
Led astray by the pixies
If someone drinks too much and gets – as we say in Ashburton – *shamfered up* (drunk), and their feet go backwards but they want to go forwards, they are accused of being 'pixie led'.

PLANCIN, PLANCHEEN
Planking, floorboards
Also pronounced 'planchin':
'I have always been the one that has had to scrub the planchin, which is why I suffer with housemaid's knee!'

PRANG A hay fork with two prongs

POOK Haycock – a pile of hay after it has been 'tedded' (turned), which is collected and made into a rick

POPPLES Pebbles
This word, according to 'The Oracle' at Exeter, comes from the Old English word 'papolstanus' and is said to be the name for the noise of water running over stones. It can be seen in names such as Newton Poppleford (a new town next to a poppled ford).

PUSKY Short of breath
'Caw my dear soul, Maister be praaper pusky smornin.'

QUAAZY Unwell
'Poor cheal be terrible quaazy 'n looks like 'ee be about t' hand 'een 'ees knife 'n fork!'

QUAIL Give up; eg, grass left in the sun becomes scorched and will soon get *quailed up*

QUILLAWAY A very old word used in the Plymouth area for a sty on the eyelid

RABBIN' URDICK Robin redbreast

RAIMID Stretched

RAYMES Skeleton, remains of something
'Yer 'tiz buye, zee what 'ee kin do with th' raymes o' thikky chicken.'

RIMLETS Remnants
'Do 'ee pick up all they rimlets, cheal, 'tiz like a jumble sale 'n yer.'

RUMMAGE Rubbish, junk, nonsense, have a good sort through
'Get rid o' this yer rummage will 'ee' – 'Get out, 'ee be talkin' a parcel o' ole rummage' – 'Get 'een thikky shed buye, will 'ee,'n have a rummage dru 'n zee if 'ee kin find ort?'

SCARIFY To scratch or to break up ground, to cultivate

SCAT Throw, cast, scatter
You sometimes hear *'A good scat o' rain'*; also you could scat (throw) something away and if you broke something, it could be said that you *scat 'n abroad.*

SCUMMER Fidget

SHIPPEN Milking shed

SHORDS, SHERDS, SHARDS, SHEVVERS
Small pieces of broken pottery

SKRIDDICK, SCRIDDICK
Bits and pieces, scrap
'Will 'ee pick up thikky ole skriddicks maid, 'tiz makin' the plaace look praper bissly.'

SKRITCH Screech, scream, cry

SKRITCH OWL Tawny owl

SLAMMICK, SLUMMICK, SLOMMICK
Untidy, sluggish
'Did'ee zee thikky cheal slummickin' about?'

SMITCH, SMEECH Small bits of burnt material floating about; also sometimes used for smoke

SMITCHER Frying pan
'Yer buye, scat thikky bacon 'n the ole smitcher will 'ee, I be veelin' praper leary.'

SPLITS Baps, cut rounds

SPUDDLE Potter about, move feebly

SQUAAL Squeel
'Yer will 'ee listen to 'ee squaalin.'

STOGGED, STUGGED
Bogged, unable to move

STROIL Couch grass

SUENT	Smooth *'Caw I tell 'ee maid, thikky tay went down praaper suent.'*
TAFFITY	Dainty, fussy about food *'Get on 'n aite yer grub cheal, you be praaper taffity.'*
TALLET	Loft of a building, top shelf in a barn *'I expect most of 'ee ave bin up 'n a tallet 'n made thikky pellum fall!'*
THIKKY	This, that, the, those *'Caw kin 'ee mind thikky ole maid who live up nap o' ole hill? My dear zaw, 'er walked zo many times t' thikky market 'er was purt near pummal vooted!'*
THRAIPIN'	Thrashing, good sort out, shake up *'I tell 'ee my boody, 'tiz 'bout time you give thikky cheal a good thraipin'.'*

THUNGY	Tough, dough-like substance – for example, putty
THURDLE GUTTED	Thin, starved *'You'm lookin' praaper thurdle gutted buye, do 'ee ave zome o' this yer teddy cake – 'twill make 'ee graw thicker.'*
TIDDLY TOPE	Wren
TIFFLES, TIFFLINS	Bits of cotton, lint *'Yer maid, yer dress be vull o' tifflins, get yerzel yer 'n yer what I be tellin' to 'ee, yu'm aidin' towards a good thraipin'.'*
TILTH	Broken down soil, ready for tilling
TITTYMAL	Titmouse
TIZZICK	Sick, unwell *'Caw my dear zaw, father be praper tizzicky.'*

TOAD RIDDINS	Frog spawn; I have also heard it called *toad Riddlins.*
TOM NODDY	Tadpole *If someone was said to be 'tom noddy' they were being described as having a 'big aid 'n no body'.*
TRAPSE	Drag feet when walking Children, when they do not want to go on a walk, will trapse about, dragging their heels: *'Caw will 'ee look at thikky cheel trapsen' 'bout.'*
UZ	Us, we
UZ BE	We are
UZ BETTER WAY	We better had
UZ EVE	We have
UZ'L	We will
UZ IZ	We are How to use the above in a sentence? Simple, try this: *'Uz be gwain to, cuz uz be aidin' fer trouble, cuz uz eve done it once 'n uz'l do it again, uz ad better way, anyhow!'*
VAUCHIN'	Move fast *'Caw will 'ee look at thikky cheal, 'ee be vauchin' 'ee's bike like a maizound* [mad dog]*'.*
VEAR	Suckling pig
VEESH	Fish I love to go fishing; trouble is I usually end up with a 'Saltash rig' (*wet ass 'n no veesh*).
VIDDY, VITTY	Well, all right, correct *''Ow be knackin' vore?' 'Oh I be purt viddy, me boody.'*
VIZGIE	A double-bladed digging tool with one horizontal blade and one vertical blade; also sometimes called a 'two bill' Anyone know any other names for it?
VORES	Furrows; according to 'The Oracle' at Exeter, this is a 14th-century word.
VUZKITE	Kestrel
VUZZ	Furze, gorse *'If you'm gwain up Dartmoor with yer "fern ticket" make sure you dawnt rin into any vuzz bushes.'*
WANT	Mole

WANTNAP Molehill

WAPS Wasp

WERTS, WORTS, URTS
Whortleberries. Another name I have heard them called by her indoors is 'wertle bertles' but then again the missus is from North Devon! In Ashburton they are always referred to as 'urts' And don't forget if you are going picking urts, take your 'fern ticket' with you.

WHIPS 'N WHILE
Now and again, occasionally
''Ee's stickin' 'ees aid 'een 'n out, ivery whips 'n while, jist like a viddler's elbow.'
'Uz'l eve t' zee 'n ivery whips 'n while, cuz if uz dawnt, uz'l niver caal t' mind what 'n looks like!'

WINNARD Heron

YAFFERS 'N YAWS Heifers and ewes

YER Year, hear, here, ear
The best example I know of this is simply: *'Yer Maister, will 'ee put yer yer yer 'n yer what you kin yer, cuz yer yerin's better 'n mine!'*

YERD TELL Heard tell
'Well, I've yerd tell that ole mother zo 'n zo be praaper tizzicky!'

YORKS Leather (or binder twine if you are not that rich!), tied just below the knees to help keep your trousers out of the mud or suchlike.

ZACKLY Exactly

ZAMZAWED Tea that has been stewed is said to be zamzawed

ZAMZODDEN, ZAMSOWDEN
Overcooked or undercooked

ZEX Six
Wan; dree; vower; vive; zex; zeb'm; leb'm

ZOWPEG, ZOWPIG Woodlouse; also sometimes called a *chuggy pig* (North Devon)

ZUGS Bogs, soft ground (see also **'Stogged, Stugged'**)

ZWANT Soft, pliable

A Local Look at Nursery Rhymes

Humpty Dumpty

A Deb'm Alphabet

A	APPLE	*As red as a rawze (rose)*
B	BULE	*With a ring droo 'ees nawze (nose)*
C	COW	*Vull o' 'ees own charm (full of her own charm)*
D	DUMPLIN	*Deb'm volk oo wont do 'ee no harm*
E	EDIFICATION	*Make 'ee wise at th' end o' th' day*
F	FINNIKY	*Zome maid who dawnt like rompin' 'n thikky hay*
G	GRANFER GRIGG	*With 'ees bandy ole legs*
H	HEN	*A layin' o' thikky eggs*
I	IVERY WHIPS 'N WHILE	*Meanin' now 'n agaan (again)*
J	JUNKET	*Like Mother maaks, 'twill niver be th' zaam*
K	KITTY TOPE	*A Jenny wren gatherin' grub*
L	LEARY	*Why dawnt 'ee ev a pasty in a pub?*
M	MUMP AID	*'Ee got th' brains o' a brick wall*
N	NORT	*Meanin' nothing at all*
O	OSSES	*Worrited be vlies*
P	PELLUM	*Layin' down 'n thikky sties*
Q	QUAZZY	*Veelin' really unwell*
R	RAWZE	*Kin' 'ee call to mind th' smell?*
S	SCRUMPY	*Th' West Countryman's liquor*
T	TEDDY CAAKE	*'Twill make 'ee graw thicker*
U	UPITTY	*Tempers grawin' quite large*
V	VARMER	*Th' aid man in charge*
W	WANTNAP	*A place fer piskies t' squat*
X	?	*'Tiz fer zummat, but I'm blawed if I knaw what!*
Y	YOKEL	*A bloke o' th' land*
Z	ZUMMER	*When 'thikky countryzide's grand*

Country Sayings

These old sayings are often heard – perhaps you may find a use for them:

- **''Erv only give 'n a squat 'n a bruise'** meaning clothing that has not been ironed very well.
- **'Like a tawd 'n a bucket'** meaning somebody who does not know which way to turn.
- **'You look like you bin' put 'n with thikky braad 'n took out with thikky cake'** 'You look like you have been put in with the bread and taken out with the cake', meaning half baked!
- **'You brake yer leg me boody, dawnt 'ee come rinnin to me'** '(If) you break your leg my beautiful, don't you come running to me'.
- **''Ee's es much use es a dug with zide pockets'** – no bliddy use to anybody.
- **'Nawse like a jug andle'**, meaning a big nose.
- **'Neck like a swanner duck'**, meaning a long neck.
- **'I knaw 'ee's in there cuz I zeed'n come out.'**
- **'H'apenny aid 'n varthin' tailed'** 'Halfpenny head and farthing tailed', meaning with a new hat but down at heel.
- **''Tiz cold enough fer a fur linned walkin' stick.'**
- **'You dree's a right pair, if you want to stay yer, you better get out.'**
- **'Cream on pilchards'**, meaning nice clean coat over dirty clothing.
- **''Tiz blawin' nough ver to blaw thikky teeth off a zaw.'**

A young lady wearing a very tight pair of jeans passes a couple of locals stood yappin' and after they watch her walk down the road for a while, one man turns to the other and says:

> **'Caw my dear days, 'tiz jist like a couple o' verrets in a rat catcher's bag.'**

The same two locals are walking along a street and one of them notices someone continually peering out the side of the curtains, watching them. One turns to the other and says:

> **'Will 'ee look to 'er, there's more eyes on 'er than there is in a zack o' teddies.'**
> (I think these days they call it Neighbourhood Watch!)

HORNED RABBIT – this was a poacher's name for venison. If you got caught, you would say:

> **'Zorry yer 'onner, I thought 'twas 'n 'orned rabbit.'**

LONG TAILED RABBIT – pheasant. This expression was often used by someone who shot a pheasant while out shooting rabbits. He would say to the policeman or farmer:

> **'I'm zorry yer 'onner, but I thought 'twas a long tailed rabbit.'**

Riddles n' Rooks

I have been asked what 'Devon Wind Suckers' are. These are people who, when wishing to express acknowledgement that they have heard what is being said, but really not wanting to give you a response or answer, will nod their head upwards and give a short draw of breath inwards. This can mean whatever you, or they, want it to mean!

Contrary Woman – I know there is no such thing but the late Nancy Boyce gave me this description some years ago:

> **'If ever 'er say's 'er will, 'er won't. If ever 'er say's 'er won't, 'er will. 'N 'er did.'**

A farmer wins a toilet brush in one of the many coffee morning draws held in his local town and when asked two weeks later how he is getting on with the brush he says:

> **'Terrible buye, I wish I niver set eyes on the blessed thing. I ended up gettin' so sore usin' 'n, that I had to go back to usin' toilet paper!'**

An old farmer goes to the doctor because he has terrible stomach trouble and after a good examination all over, the consultation continues:

> **Doctor: 'Are you regular?'**
> **Farmer: ''Eys zir, 7.30 every mornin', niver missed in 75 yers.'**
> **Doctor: 'Well that can't be the trouble then.'**
> **Farmer: 'That's what you think maister, zee I dawnt get up till 9.30.'**

How can you tell the difference between rooks and crows? It's very easy:

> **'If there's more than two rooks in a field, they'm crows and if there's more than two crows in a field, they'm rooks.'**

I hope that helps explain it.

CHAPTER 2

Yerd Tell in Ashburton

I talk about Ashburton a lot as this is the place where I live so obviously I am a little biast! I can tell you that throughout the whole of Devon there are many customs and traditions that are still carried on and here are a few of them. If you are visiting any town in Devon, it is worth logging on to its web site for details of events taking place.

Not only am I biast about Ashburton, my birth place, but I am just as passionate about Devon which, in my opinion, is HEAVEN ON EARTH.

Ashburton's Portreeve

The ancient Saxon position of Portreeve is an important part of Ashburton's history and is still preserved today. Dating back to AD 820, the office is the only one now held by Act of Parliament, although it exists in eight other towns in England.

The chief duty of a Saxon Portreeve was to represent the king in legal transactions and he was often the only person who could read and write, especially when all legal documents were in Latin.

Today's Portreeve is upholding an old tradition and he is still appointed with his Bailiff, Ale Tasters, Bread Weighers and other ancient offices, although the position now mainly involves acting as a social head for the town and attending the many charity events that take place in Ashburton. Each year in St Lawrence Chapel on the fourth Tuesday in November, at 4 pm, the courts assemble and all jury members are sworn into office along with the Portreeve and Bailiff. The juries also make 'presentments'; these can be very varied and the Steward to the Courts subsequently despatches each of them to the relevant authorities, people or organisations.

The Court Leet elects the Portreeve, who is then sworn in at this ceremony and the Foreman makes presentments on matters of local interest. This court is composed of freeholders of the town and also elects other offices, such as the

The Master Bailiff, Michael J. Lowrey (left) and the 1187th Portreeve, John L. Germon.

Ale Tasters, Bread Weighers, Constables, the Inspector of Trees and the Bearer of Evergreen.

The Court Baron is made up of tenants of the town; they elect Constables, Marshalls, Viewers of the Market, Viewers of Water Courses, Searchers and Sealers of Leather, Scavengers and Pig Drovers, and the Foreman of the Baron Jury also makes presentments.

One event that occurs annually is the ancient Ale Tasting and Bread Weighing Ceremony, which takes place in July. The Portreeve, Bailiff and members of the courts parade through the town and call at every public house and bakery. At the pubs the Bailiff demands that the landlord/landlady produce two tankards of their best ale so that the Ale Tasters may judge its quality. They taste it and, because of something that happened many years ago, they pour some of the ale onto a stool and then one Ale Taster wearing a leather apron sits on the stool to judge if the ale has had water added – if the apron sticks, the beer is of good quality; if it does not, it has been watered down. If the brew is considered to be of an acceptable standard it is declared so and the proprietors of the house are given a sprig of evergreen to hang on their door to show all and sundry that they sell good ale and they are also presented with a certificate. The parade then moves on to the next venue after the town crier has cried 'God save the Queen'.

At the bakeries the Bread Weighers test the bread to see if it is of good weight and if it is the Master Baker is presented with a certificate accordingly.

The Summer and Winter Carnivals

Ashburton's Summer Carnival is one of the oldest, possibly ***the*** oldest, surviving in Devon. Written records date it back to 1891, but it is believed to have been started in the mid 1880s to raise funds for a new hospital. It takes place during June/July and ten days of activities culminate in a grand

The Saturday Draw Sellers – a mad gang who enter into the spirit of the carnival every year.

procession of floats on the first Saturday in July, when the whole town gets involved.

The main function of the carnival is to raise money for local charities, town groups and clubs. This ensures widespread local support. Ashburton also holds a Winter Carnival in November, which is also a very popular event and a great spectacle.

Cutty Dyer

Ashburton's most famous myth is that of Cutty Dyer, an evil little water sprite that lives in the river Ashburn under King's Bridge, next to the town hall. For many generations naughty children were warned to keep away or he would cut their throats and drink their blood. As a youngster I remember running very fast past King's Bridge, especially when it was getting dimpsy, for fear of 'Cutty Dyer'. Misbehaving children were not his sole targets – he also took action against those folk who drank too much. He would eagerly waylay anyone in a state of alcoholic stupor as they staggered home, and they could expect the same blood-letting treatment.

The Black Dogs of Devon

The county has many legends of 'Black Dogs' and there are plenty of tales told about them. In Down St Mary, north-west of Crediton, it is said that many villagers have seen a Black Dog at night, being very noisy as it passes the old smithy and goes through the churchyard. One resident told how he and his friends heard the Black Dog coming and, being scared, they hid in a field and watched it go past. It was very large, about the size of a calf, with shiny eyes and was baying.

In St Giles in the Wood, in the north of the county, it was considered very unlucky to mention the Black Dog, and if they heard anyone talking about it they would turn away. One of the first sightings was in the mid 18th century when a young girl was walking home from church with one of her parents. A great Black Dog, with shiny eyes came from behind them. The girl was very scared and grabbed her parent's hand. They walked on without speaking and the dog ran alongside them for quite some time until it disappeared. Many people in St Giles in the Wood have spotted the Black Dog but few are willing to talk abut it.

There have been sightings in Barnstaple, Torrington, Copplestone, Crediton and Exeter so if you are in any of these areas at night, keep an eye out!

Honiton Hot Pennies

Honiton in East Devon is not only famous for its lace but also for an old custom that takes place there in July – the annual Honiton Hot Pennies Day.

The town crier holds a floral pole which is topped off with a golden glove. This is paraded around in front of the crowds, with the announcement 'The glove is up, God save the Queen'. This signifies that the Honiton Fair has commenced. The crowds gather round and wait in anticipation for the 'Hot Pennies' which are thrown from the windows of the town's hostelries.

I have been told that the custom dates back to when the wealthy residents of Honiton would 'aid' the poor or less fortunate of the town. It is said that the pennies were hot because the people who threw them took great delight in watching the peasants burn their hands as they scrambled to collect the money.

The annual fair at Honiton is of very long standing and the right to hold a fair was granted to the residents in the 13th century.

The Ashen Faggot

Many traditions have disappeared over the years but one that you can still come across is the burning of the 'Ashen Faggot' which dates back to very early times.

On Christmas Eve the Ashen Faggot would be placed on the great hearth; they varied in size according to the size of the fireplace, some could be up to five feet long and around twenty inches thick. They were securely bound with several strong binds of hazel and the bundle was usually green ash. Every time a bind burnt through and broke all those present would raise their glasses and drink their cider or beer.

In some areas they would sit a child on the faggot until one of the binds broke or as long as the youngster would be prepared to sit there, apparently this tested the nerve and timidity of the child and was also a good indicator of the pluck of the youngster for the future.

Turning the Devil's Stone

On 5th November, in the small village of Shebbear in North Devon, there takes place the very old custom of turning the devil's stone. On that day, local people gather at a large oak tree near to St Michael's church where a huge stone lies. Bell ringers ring out the bells, usually in a disorderly peal so that the noise will drive out the Devil. The stone is then turned using metal bars.

How the stone came to be there is a mystery. One story is that it was dropped by the Devil when he was cast out of heaven. Others think it may have been an

Turning the Stone (courtesy of www.shebbearvillage.co.uk).

altar stone used by those who worshipped Teutonic gods. Whatever the origin of the stone, it was believed that if this ancient ceremony of turning the stone was not performed, the village and surrounding district would suffer misfortune.

Ottery St Mary Tar Barrels Ceremony

Otter St Mary in East Devon is internationally famous for its Tar Barrel ceremony. This very old custom, which takes place in November, is said to have originated in the 17th century. Outside public houses tar soaked barrels which can weigh up to 30 kilos are lit and, with flames pouring from the barrels, they are lifted and carried around the town. Great friendships are formed by the barrel carriers as they jostle to take turns. Many generations of the same families have carried on the tradition and do so with great pride. There are conflicting opinions as to how and why the ceremony began. Generally it is believed it was a pagan ritual performed to rid the town of evil spirits.

Age is no barrier at the Tar Barrels ceremony.

The streets and side roads are packed with people who come to watch this amazing spectacle. The barrels eventually end up at a very large bonfire next to the river Otter and if you are able to witness this event, you will not be disappointed.

A Local Look at Nursery Rhymes

Little Miss Muffet

CHAPTER 3

'Gwain Abroad?' No, Gwain Maize!

My first visit to France was when the Ashburton Twinning Association celebrated its 10th anniversary with Cleder, their twin town; they suggested that as I was Portreeve, I should go to visit Cleder. Well, I was not too certain, especially as I get seasick just having a bath! Anyway, I decided that it was my duty as Portreeve to go and I did. On my return, I thought that I should write down my experience and whilst some of the following story is true, some of it ... well let's just put it down as poetic licence.

'If you'm gwain to France, you have to git yourzelf a passport,' said the missus.

'What do 'ee mean a passport?' I says.

'Oh 'tiz a little ole book that you puts yer photo 'een 'n writes who you be 'n whereabouts you comes from.'

'What the hang fer?' I says. 'I knaws who I be and where I comes from.'

'Well you might maister, but thikky ole French dawnt!'

'Well 'tiz nort to do with they,' I says.

'Well you got to have one and that's that. Get it done.'

Well if 'er indoors says get it done, trust me, you get it done!

Next 'er said, 'Now you got to go 'n git youzelf some money.'

'What fer?' I says. 'I already got some.'

'That i'dn no gude, yer gurt vule.'

'Why not? Tev bin good enough fer hundreds o' yers so far.'

'No,' says the missus, 'tev got to be French money.'

Well by this time I was beginning to wish I'd never o' said I would go.

Anyhow, off I goes to the ole bank and I says to the maid behind the fence, 'I'd like zome money to go to France with, if you please.'

'Certainly zur,' 'er says, 'would 'ee like francs?'

'MY GURD NO,' I says, 'let 'ee git 'ees awn. I got enough problems lookin' avter mezelf!'

Well that made the ole maid behind the fence laaf, though I still i'dn quite sure why. Anyhows out I comes with me money.

'Right,' says the missus with a termined look on 'er face, 'off you goes now 'n git yer hair cut.'

'WHAAT,' I says, 'I only had it cut 'bout dree weeks agone.'

'You git it cut,' 'er says, 'n if 'er says get it cut, you get it cut!

Next day uz was up brave 'n early, cases packed 'n on our way to Plymouth. Caw, 'twas a master big boat, they called 'n a furry, 'n I was most amazed how idle zome volks be. Do 'ee knaw, zome of em even had to drive their cars on thikky ole boat, cuz they was too idle to walk on 'n. I noticed on this yer boat that they had a bar, so I says to the missus how I thought 'twas about time uz bad ourselves a drink! So uz sits down at this yer bar 'n avter about dree t' vower pints I started to notice how the zea was tryin' to overtaake the ole boat, then twude try to go back to the plaace where 'ee'd just come from. Next, twude decide to try 'n git on top of 'n, then next time twude try 'n duck under 'n. Well, I kin tell 'ee that was 'nough fer me! All at once me stummick decided 'ee'd try 'n do the saame, one minute 'twas down at me ankles 'n the next minute 'twas tryin' to come out droo the top o' me aid. CAW MY DEAR ZAW, I thought I was gwain turn inzides out. That's the trouble when you try's to drink foreign Scrumpy 'zee, tid'n no gude fer 'ee.

Anyhow all at once uz wuz there, Frenchland. Uz soon parked up the 'ole boat 'n was on our way out, when all at once some blawk with a station maister's hat on says, ''Ev 'ee anythin' to declare zur?'

'Well, only that I had me hair cut yesterday maister.'

'No,' 'ee says, ''ev 'ee got ort in yer cases?'

Well what a maize question I thought to mezelf, as if I'd bring 'n empty suitcase all the way to Frenchland fer nort!

'Course I 'ev,' I says, so the next thing 'ee does is opens up the cases 'n starts having a good ferrit round to see what 'ee could vind. Then 'ee gits out a bit o' chalk 'n starts to draw all over me case.

'Yer,' I says, 'if you want to do some drawin' you git yourzelf a pen 'n a bit o' paper 'n a proper manner.'

Well uz evenually gits passed ole station maister, and ketches sight of the French volks. Well you never will guess what happen' next. A gurt French blawk 'bout dree furlongs high, with hands like sledge hammers, puts both 'ees gurt hands on me shoulders 'n starts to kiss me; I would'n mind but 'ee even closed 'ees eyes 'n looked like 'ee was enjoying it! Well that done it fer me, now I was completely confussed, 'n on me way back to thikky ole boat.

The missus said, 'Where be gwain?'

The President of the Cleder Twinning Association holding up the Devon flag.

''Ome,' I says.

I kin tell 'ee now that the next time somebody says to me 'I'm gwain abroad fer 'n holiday,' I shill tell 'n straight, 'You take my advice maister 'n stay 'ome yer, cuz I dawnt knaw 'bout gwain abroad my boodie, you'm more likely to end up GWAIN MAIZE.'

I have to admit, at first I was very English and as soon as I came to a French man, out would shoot my arm in readiness to shake his hand – that way I would not have to kiss him. These days and after a couple bottles of the local lemonade, I really do not give a damn, and have enjoyed many a good time with our friends in Cleder, even if they do talk funny!

CHAPTER 4

Countree Cures – Advice for the Tizzicky

All these cures are recorded from the 1800s. I cannot promise they work and certainly do not advise you try them – but if you do, it is at your own risk! Some of them really take some stomaching and it is sobering to consider how common ailments used to be treated in days gone by.

CHILBLAINS

- Waysh yer veet 'n waater that 'ev jist come vrum boiled teddies.
- It was long believed that a good thrashing on the feet with holly was an excellent cure – 'cured but unable to walk'. Or as Jan Stewer would say: 'Pummel voted fer a fortnight.'

COLDS

- If you want to sweat out a cold, pick elderberry flowers, place them in a bag and leave them to dry out. Once dried, boil them in water then strain the liquid and drink like you would tea.

EARACHE

- Take a loaf of wheaten bread hot from the oven, divide it into two and apply to both yer 'oles as hot as you can bear; bind them and this will cause perspiration and by the help of God, you will no longer have earache.

JAUNDICE

- Boil 4 oz of fresh dandelion roots in two pints of water until the liquid is reduced to one pint; strain off and take a wine glassful, twice a day.

PNEUMONIA

- Mustard powder wetted and mixed with honey and spread on brown paper. Take the mixture and apply to the chest as a poultice.

SORE THROAT

- Take a cabbage leaf, boil it, then add honey to the juice that is left, then drink.

STIES

- Take the hair from a horse's forelock and eat it on wheaten bread. (This one's not for me!)
- Rub the sty with a gold wedding ring.
- Find a jet-black cat and take some hair from its front left leg when there is a full moon; brush this along the sty, working from the nose to the ear.

SUNBURN

- 2 lb of elderflowers simmered in 2 lb of drippin' until crisp then sieve out the fat and rub this on the affected area; this will ease the uncomfortable burn being experienced.

WARTS

- Rub warts with a radish or juice of marigold flowers.
- Apply the milky sap from dandelion flowers.
- Cut off the head of an eel, rub the raw end of the head over the wart then bury the head of the eel and as the head rots away so the wart will disappear.

- It was strongly believed in 1898 that if you touched the eye of a wart with a coat of a man who never saw his father, this was a sure cure.

WHOOPING COUGH

- Carry the afflicted child into a sheepfold and let the sheep breathe on its face, then lay the child down on the spot of ground from which a sheep has just risen. Continue this daily for one week.

FOR SUFFERERS OF BAD WIND

- Mix together ½ pint of milk and four teaspoonfuls of very fine soot, and drink freely.

BOILS

- Apply a plaister of honey and wheatflour
- Drink dock or elder tea
- Apply to the body salt bacon; this is a sure cure for boils (allegedly)

HOW TO CATCH FLEAS

- This is a well-tried method if you want to ketch fleas in your bed (1898). Remove the bedclothes VERY GENTLY. Take a bar of soap that has been soaked and is a bit 'cledgy', hold it above the flea and slowly move down towards it. Don't worry if the flea jumps as it will hit the soap and the job is done anyway, but if it does not jump then when you are just above it, drop the bar of soap on top of it and when you lift up the soap you will have got your flea stuck firmly.

Boodiful!

A Local Look at Nursery Rhymes

Little Jack Horner

CHAPTER 5

A Devonshire Song Book

Devon has many songs and some are written in dialect which is very interesting when you try to sing them as written. I find that if you have a couple of pints of scrumpy, this helps to understand them easier!

This is one of the most famous songs of Devon; words by Edward Boulton, early 1900s:

GLORIOUS DEVON

Coombe and Tor, green meadow and lane,
Birds on the waving bough,
Beetling cliffs by the surging main,
Rich red loam for the plough;
Devon's the fount of the bravest blood,
That braces England's breed,
Her maidens fair as the apple bud,
And her men are men indeed.
When Adam and Eve were dispossess'd
Of the garden hard by heaven,
They planted another one down in the West,
'Twas Devon, glorious Devon.

Spirits of old-world heroes wake,
By river and cove and hoe,
Grenville, Hawkins, Raleigh and Drake,
And a thousand more we know;
To ev'ry land the wide-world o'er
Some slips of the old stock roam,
Leal friends in peace, dread foes in war,
With hearts still true to home.

Old England's counties by the sea
From East to West are seven,
But the gem of that fair galaxy
Is Devon, glorious Devon.

Dorset, Somerset, Cornwall, Wales,
May envy the likes of we,
For the flow'r of the West, the first, the best,
The pick of the bunch us be;
Squab pie, junket and cyder brew,
Richest of cream from the cow,
What 'ud Old England without 'em do?
And where 'ud 'un be to now?
As crumpy as a lump of lead
Be a loaf without good leaven,
And the yeast Mother England do use for her bread
Be Devon, glorious Devon.

This is another good Devon song and I think the best version I ever heard was sung by Geoffrey Hannaford at one of the Ashburton Devon Dialect Club's events:

THE FARMER'S BOY

The sun had sunk behind the hill, across yon dreary moor,
When wet and cold there came a boy up to the farmer's door;
'Can you tell me,' said he, 'if any there be, who would like to give employ
To plough and to sow, to reap and to mow,
To be a farmer's boy, to be a farmer's boy?'

'My father's dead, my mother's left with four poor children small,
And what is worse for mother still, I'm the eldest of them all;
But tho' little, I'll work as hard as I can, if I can be employed
To plough and to sow, to reap and to mow,
To be a farmer's boy, to be a farmer's boy.'

The farmer's wife cries, 'Try the lad, let him no further seek.'
'Oh do, Papa!' the daughter cries, while tears roll down her cheek;
'For those that will work, 'tis hard to want or to wander for employ,
To plough and to sow, to reap and to mow,
To be a farmer's boy, to be a farmer's boy.'

'But if no boy you chance to want, one favour I've to ask,
To shelter me till dawn of day, from the cold wintry blast;
At the break of day I'll trudge away, elsewhere to seek employ,
To plough and to sow, to reap and to mow,
To be a farmer's boy, to be a farmer's boy.'

The farmer's boy he grew a man, the good old farmer died;
He left the lad with all he had, and daughter for his bride;
The boy that was, now a farmer is, and he thinks and smiles with joy,
And he blesses the day, when he passed that way,
To be a farmer's boy, to be a farmer's boy.

Finally, this song, closely associated with Widecombe Fair held annually in September, goes back in its present form to 1890 when the Rev. Baring Gould published it in his *Songs of the West*:

WIDECOMBE FAIR

Tom Pierce, Tom Pierce lend me your grey mare,
All along, down along, out along lee.
For I want to go to Widecombe Fair,
Wi' Bill Brewer, Jan Stewer, Peter Gurney,
Peter Davy, Dan'l Whiddon, Harry Hawk,
Old Uncle Tom Cobley and all, Old Uncle Tom Cobley and all.

And when shall I see again my grey mare?
All along, down along, out along lee.
By Friday soon or Saturday noon,
Wi' Bill Brewer, Jan Stewer ... etc.

Old Uncle Tom Cobley and all (Don Osmond)

Then Friday came and Saturday noon,
All along, down along, out along lee.
Tom Pierce's old mare hath not trotted home,
Wi' Bill Brewer, Jan Stewer ... etc.

So Tom Pierce he got up to the top of the hill,
All along, down along, out along lee.
And he see'd his old mare a-making her will,
Wi' Bill Brewer, Jan Stewer ... etc.

So Tom Pierce's old mare, her took sick and died,
All along, down along, out along lee.
And Tom he sat down on a stone and he cried,
Wi' Bill Brewer, Jan Stewer ... etc.

But this isn't the end of this shocking affair,
All along, down along, out along lee.
Nor, though they be dead, of the horrid career
Of Bill Brewer, Jan Stewer ... etc.

When the wind whistles cold on the moor of a night,
All along, down along, out along lee.
Tom Pierce's ole mare doth appear gashly white,
Wi' Bill Brewer, Jan Stewer ... etc.

And all the long night be heard skirling and groans,
All along, down along, out along lee.
From Tom Pierce's old mare in her rattlin' bones
And from Bill Brewer, Jan Stewer, Peter Gurney,
Peter Davy, Dan'l Whiddon, Harry Hawk,
Old Uncle Tom Cobley and all, Old Uncle Tom Cobley and all.

A friend of mine, Peter, asked me the question one day, 'Who is me?' I pass this question on to you: Who is the 'me' in the song?

CHAPTER 6

'Cakes 'n Scrumpy!' – A Taste of the County

These are recipes given to me by friends and relatives who for many years have enjoyed the end product. You will notice that 'scrumpy' and 'cider' appear in some of them – these are two different things. Scrumpy, in my opinion, is the only one to have, but beware you do not become 'pixie laid'n'.

MOUTH SPAICH USEFUL EXPRESSIONS

Why not try some of the following next time you are doing some cooking? You never know, they may help the recipes turn out better.

Dollop A Devonshire measurement. Dollop een a bit more buye!

Hang the blessed thing!

Strapper Hanger on, someone who hasn't been invited to eat.

Thraipin' A good sort out, i.e. mix well.

Tid'n gwain right, I better ave another daish o' scrumpy.

When 'ees brown 'ees right, when 'ees burnt 'ees *******!**
No good at all!

Yers one I maid ealier
(I got that one from Blue Peter.)

Aunty Mary's Harvest Puddin'

Slices of buttered bread
1 lb cooking apples
2 oz suet
3 oz brown sugar
3 oz seedless raisins
1 oz chopped nuts
2 eggs
Grated lemon rind
1 cup milk
Caster sugar

Grease and line a dish with the buttered bread. Slice the apples and mix with the suet, raisins, nuts, sugar and lemon rind. Fill the pie dish with the mixture and cover with more buttered bread. Beat eggs, add to the milk and pour over the top. Cover and stand for 1½ hours or overnight. Bake in a moderate oven 350°F/180°C (gas mark 4) for 1 hour. Sprinkle with caster sugar and serve.

As Aunty Mary in the Ashburton Deb'm Dialect Club always reminds me: 'Dawn 'ee forget thikky clotted cream, Jan.'

Avril's Pork Pie

7 pork chops (boned)
4 medium onions (sliced)
2 leeks (thinly sliced)
Salt & pepper
9 oz pastry
7 medium apples (sliced)
1 small dollop of nutmeg, all spice & five spice
2¼ tbs sugar
1½ pints of scrumpy

If chops are very large, cut in half. Layer ingredients – chops first with a layer of sliced apple, sprinkle with part of the spices and sugar, top these with the onions, leeks, etc. repeat this until all the ingredients are used up. Pour on the scrumpy and then place on the pastry. Brush over with milk. Cover with foil and cook at around 300°F/150°C (gas mark 2) for 1¼ –1½ hours.

This one is from the mother-in-law – you know, the one I'm always on about, in the nicest possible way, of course. Mind you, she always has 2 pints of scrumpy – uses 1½ pints and drinks the other half.

Bill's Deb'm Pudding

¾ cup breadcrumbs
3 separated eggs
½ tsp ground cinnamon
¼ pint clotted cream
½ cup shelled almonds
6 oz caster sugar
1 tsp grated lemon rind
1 cup cider

Stand breadcrumbs in a warm place to dry slightly. Put almonds through a mincer; beat egg yolks, add sugar and beat until fluffy. Stir in the crumbs, almonds, cinnamon and lemon rind. Beat egg whites until stiff and fold into the mixture. Turn lightly into a buttered cake tin with a removable base. Bake in a moderate oven 350°F/180°C (gas mark 4) for 35–40 minutes, until firm. Remove from the oven and stand for a minute or two. Slip off gently onto a flat, hot dish. Serve with cream, also the hot cider.

Don't worry about yer diet after eat'n this, maid. 'Twill feel anzum!

Cider Cake

4 oz sugar
4 oz butter
2 eggs
8 oz sifted flour
1 tsp bicarb of soda
½ tsp nutmeg
2 teacups cider or more

First cream the butter and the sugar and the well-beaten eggs. Sift half the flour, soda and nutmeg into the mixture. Stir the cider to foam and slowly pour over the ingredients. Pour in the remaining flour and thoroughly mix. Bake in a greased tin for about 45 minutes in a moderate oven.

If you use more than 2 teacups of scrumpy, well you'm greedy!

Deb'm Savoury Pasty

3/4 lb damsons
3 tbs water
1 finely chopped onion
12 oz chopped cooked pork
Water to mix
1 beaten egg
Seasoning
1/2 tsp nutmeg
9 oz flour
2 oz margarine
2 oz cooking fat

Stone and wash the damsons; place the fruit into a saucepan with the water and nutmeg. Stew gently until cooked. Mix the onion and the pork, and season to taste. Sift the flour and a pinch of salt, and rub in all the fats. Give it a good thraipin' till smooth, then dollop this on a floured board and cut into 6 circles. Drain the damsons and mix the fruit with the pork. Put a small dollop of the mixture in the centre of each circle, fold in half and dampen the edges to seal. Brush the pasties with beaten egg. Bake in a moderate oven for 1/2 hour (ish).

Petroc Trelawney note: A DEVON pasty!

Devonshire Splits

Just the thing for when you've got boodiful weather 'n a deesh o' tay

1/2 pint milk
1/4 oz dried yeast or double quantity of fresh yeast
1 tsp sugar
2 oz butter
1 lb preferably strong plain flour
1 tsp salt
1 oz caster sugar

Devonshire Splits.

To serve:
½ pint clotted cream *16 tsps strawberry jam*
Icing sugar

Warm the milk. Cream the yeast with the teaspoonful of sugar and when liquid, add half the milk at blood heat. Dissolve the butter in the remaining warm milk. Make a well in the centre of the sieved flour and salt, add the yeast mixture, milk and caster sugar, then beat well for a few minutes until smooth. Knead lightly. Cover and leave to rise until doubled in size. Turn dough onto a floured surface and divide equally into 16. Knead each piece into a ball, rolling it under your hand to make a good shape. Place on greased baking trays and leave to prove in a draught-free, warm place for about 20 minutes.

Bake in a hot oven 425°F/220°C (gas mark 7) for 15-20 minutes. They should be nicely browned and firm on the base. Cool on a wire tray. Cut one side diagonally and fill each bun with a spoonful of jam and clotted cream. Dust with icing sugar. Makes 16.

Note: this is what we had long before there were scones.

Do you put the cream first or the jam? There is a right way! Having done a rough survey, I can tell you that the majority of Deb'm folk put cream first, then the jam. In Cornwall they tend to do it the other way round – but then again, they would!

Lustleigh Truff

1 lb truff (Devon for bull trout)	*¼ lb field mushrooms*
1 oz butter (or thickish cream)	*½ tsp salt*
1 tsp parsley	*1 pint of cider*

Enough pie pastry to make two good-sized pasties

Take the truff and remove its innards. Clean the cavity with fresh water and a stiff hand brush; lay aside in a basin of cider. Chop the mushrooms into small pieces and fold them into the butter or cream, adding the parsley and salt. When a paste has been formed, remove the truff from the cider, it being well marinated if left long, and fill the stomach with the paste.

Make a pie pastry and cut into two dobs (small lumps). Roll out each piece into flats, each longer and wider than the truff by some 2 inches each side. Lay the truff on one piece then put the other on top and pleat the edges. Before putting into a hot oven make three cuts at the top. Bake until golden crisp brown (the colour can be darkened by throwing spoonfuls of salt on the fire from time to time, as with a roast). Serves 2.

Please note: this is not Stargazzy Pie. You see, that's Cornish, this idn' – 'tiz Deb'm!

Mabel Cobbledick Caake

Dedicated to Eileen Egbeare

5 oz butter or margarine
5 oz soft dark brown sugar
1 level tsp mixed spice
3 oz sultanas
14 oz jar of mincemeat
3 eggs (well beaten)
8 oz self raising flour
2 oz glace cherries (chopped)
1 oz flaked almonds

Set oven to warm – 325°F/170°C (gas mark 3). Cream butter and sugar until light and fluffy. Beat in eggs gradually, beating well between each addition. Sift flour and mixed spice into the mixture, then add the mincemeat, sultanas, almonds and cherries and mix well. Turn into an 8 inch lined and greased cake tin and bake in the centre of the oven for 1¼ –1½ hours. Test with a skewer – if the cake needs longer cooking, cover with foil to prevent over browning. This cake keeps well in an airtight tin for 2 weeks – unless you live in our house, when you're lucky if it keeps for 2 days!

Tiddy Soup – also known as Teddy Soup

(Very economical)

6 leeks peeled and thinly sliced as far as the white goes (from roots to green leaves)
4 middle-sized teddies
1 cupful rice
1 tsp salt
2 qrts water
Doorstep of bread
½ tsp pepper

The water must be completely boiling before anything is put into it; then add all of the ingredients at once, with the exception of the rice, the salt and the pepper. Cover, and let them come to a brisk boil. Add the remaining ingredients and let it all boil slowly for 1 hour, or until everything is thoroughly cooked.

Veesh Pie

(Cod in scrumpy)

1 lb cod fillet (or you can use any veesh you like)
8 mushrooms
½ pint scrumpy
1 oz butter or margarine
2 oz grated cheese
2 large tomatoes halved
Salt and pepper
1 oz plain flour

Cut cod into four and arrange in a greased oven dish with the mushrooms and tomatoes. Pour cider over and add the salt and the pepper. Bake at 375°F/190°C (gas mark 5) for about 20 minutes. Add the flour to the melted butter and cook for a few minutes. Add the liquid from the fish (make up to ½ pint with water if necessary). Bring to the boil and cook for 2–3 minutes, stirring continuously. Pour over the fish, sprinkle with grated cheese and brown under a hot grill.

That's it!!! I'm gwain out fer a pint. 'Tiz your turn to waysh up.

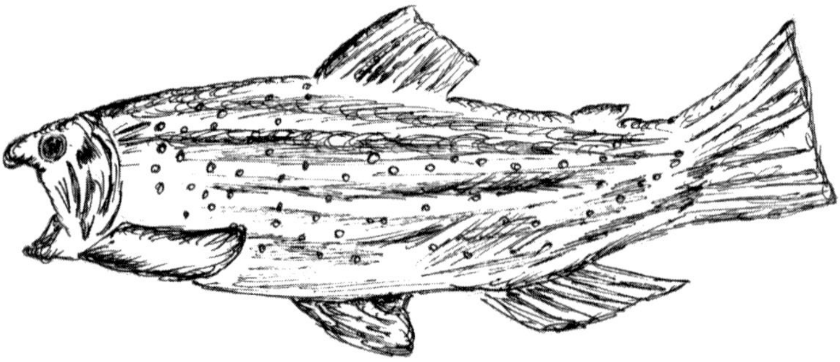

THE 'CHEERS ME BOODIES!' CARTOON HISTORY BOOK

An Almost Totally INSANE DEVONSHIRE LOOK AT British History IN PICTURES

by Richard Scollins

Alfred and the Cakes – AD 878

Canute Demonstrates His Inability to Turn the Tide – AD 1020

Lady Godiva – AD 1057

The Battle of Hastings – AD 1066

The Death of William Rufus – 1100

King John and Magna Carta - 1215

Edward I Presents His Son as Prince of Wales - 1284

Bruce and the Spider - 1306

The Battle of Agincourt – 1415

Richard III at Bosworth - 1485

Henry VIII and Anne Boleyn – 1529

Raleigh and the Puddle - 1581

Francis Drake Goes Bowling – 1588

The First Night of 'Hamlet' - 1601

The Gunpowder Plot - 1605

The Execution of Charles I - 1649

Charles II and Friends Hide From the Roundheads – 1651

Isaac Newton Discovers Gravity - 1666

Nelson at Trafalgar – 1805

Wellington Inspects His Troops – 1815

The Charge of the Light Brigade – 1854

Stanley Greets Dr Livingstone - 1871

Queen Victoria 'Not Amused' – 1878